The Best Cartoons from
THE SATURDAY EVENING POST

Compiled and edited by Steven Pettinga

ZondervanPublishingHouse
Grand Rapids, Michigan

A Division of HarperCollinsPublishers

Cartoon editor and concepts: Steven Pettinga
Art design and layout: Chris Wilhoite
Cartoon typesetters: Penny Rasdall and Phyllis Lybarger
Frontmatter typesetters: Susan Koppenol and Nancy Wilson
Executive consultant: Beurt SerVaas
Cover cartoon: Thomas Cheney
Jacket design: Mark Veldheer and Jody Langley

Printed in the United States of America

93 94 95 96 97 98 99 00 / ML / 10 9 8 7 6 5 4 3 2

Introduction

The Saturday Evening Post is the premier American showcase for single-panel cartoons and their creators. The *Post* claims that title because it remains one of the few magazines that considers everyone as its potential audience. Whether our readers are young or old, male or female, rich or poor, our intent is that they will find our cartoons upbeat, positive, insightful, and clever.

Most magazines speak to narrowly defined audiences, often poking fun at those outside their circle. Exploiting stale clichés and stereotypes makes for a cheap laugh but risks being offensive. If a *Post* reader is offended by one of our cartoons, we haven't done our job properly. We intend for our humor to be universally funny.

The *Post* is also an open book. All cartoonists are welcome. That does not mean you won't find certain cartoonists in nearly every issue. Unlike magazines that invite certain cartoonists to work for them, the *Post* does not work with a set roster of humorists and artists. The competition to be published in our pages is heated, which keeps the lineup fresh and exciting. Over 2,000 cartoons from over 200 free-lance cartoonists are reviewed for the approximately 35 cartoon slots in each issue. You have arrived when your first cartoon is published in the *Post*.

The *Post* first published cartoons in 1922 in a department titled "Short Turns and Encores," which is similar to today's "Post Scripts." But it wasn't until the highly regarded Ben Hibbs became editor in 1944 that cartoons became a vital part of the magazine. Hibbs realized the importance of cartoons for livening up text-heavy sections of the magazine. Soon, cartoons were liberally sprinkled throughout the magazine. Both readers and advertisers were pleased, and that's the way it has remained ever since.

I have nothing but the greatest respect for the cartoonists with whom I work. How difficult it must be to keep one's sense of humor in an increasingly frustrating business. Their spirit and determination are inspirational. I feel incredibly lucky to have the job I do. Even as a small child I would eagerly wait for the mailman to deliver the many magazines my parents subscribed to, and I would quickly turn to the cartoons. That excitement remains for me today.

It is a privilege to share this collection with you—to share the talent of the many great cartoonists that grace our pages. Space does not allow me to list all important contributors to this book, but I am sure that they are as proud of this collection as we are.

I hope that you enjoy this collection and have a good laugh. Laughter is good for the soul.

Steven Cornelius Pettinga
Cartoon Editor
The Saturday Evening Post

ANIMAL CRACKERS

"What can I say? They're YOU!"

WARNING! LARGE DOG CRAVING AFFECTION!

"Now, this policy will cover your home for fire, theft, flood and huffing and puffing."

JUST KIDDING

"Wanna see the hats we made out of can labels?"

"The team needs me!"

"There's the Little Dipper, there's Orion and there's the 9:30 707 to Cleveland."

"I want to impress a special boy. Got any perfume that smells like the slime monster from outer space?"

SCREEN TEST

"The following program is being brought to you by satellite..."

"Watch out, Bob, it's in a bad mode today."

"I think I've found the problem....it's not a TV, it's a microwave oven."

"We need a taller anchor man."

GOING TOO FAR

"Aren't your wake-up calls usually done over the phone?"

"Too bad George can't be here to see this."

LAUGHING
MATTERS

"All we have left now are memories, Edith.
It's a good thing I wrote them down!"

"Arnold! Will you shut that television off
and let that poor announcer go to bed!"

"How long have you been with Field and Stream?"

CHURCH CHORTLES

"Last week I did unto Billy and Marilyn Sue like you say we should, but they didn't do back to me, so next week I'm just gonna forget it!"

"Would you now please access Matthew 11:12 on your King James terminal?"

"Has anyone ever told you that you're delightfully irreverent?"

SCHOOLING AROUND

"No, you may not have your accountant call me!"

"I don't teach my students about the Bill of Rights any more—it makes them so unruly."

"It's your teacher. Quick, tell daddy to switch to PBS!"

"I learn a lot of stuff here, but it sure cuts into my day!"

"Today in school we learned the meaning of 'nervous breakdown' and 'sabbatical.'"

TIME-OUT

"Today, Brinkleyville Tech takes on Hummelstown State Teachers College, but we've got a half-time show that'll knock your socks off!"

"This is fun, Henry. Why don't you catch one?"

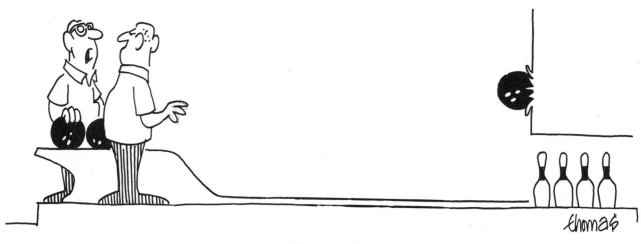

"Not so hard."

IMP-ACTS

"I didn't get the name, but the agency says the baby-sitter is a natural with children."

"We don't have any kids. Who's in there?"

"Mr. Thurlow, your child is here for a hug."

"Don't try it, son. There's not been a successful escape from here in seventeen years!"

COUNTRY CAPERS

"You're right, dear. This lens really does bring him in close."

"The piped-in music raised production, all right, but it was sheer torture milking full-grown Holsteins while they were doing the Virginia Reel."

"The lemonade should be ready. I've been feeding her lemons and sugar for a week."

"Sir, I want you to meet my daughters: Faith, Hope, Charity and Pestilence."

JASPER QUOG
MD

"I'm afraid you need a bypass—bypass
dinner and go jogging instead!"

WAISTING AWAY

"He went on a strict diet. The first
month he lost 70 pounds. The next month he
lost 60 pounds. Then he lost 50, 40, 20—and
that's the last I saw of him."

WEIGHT
&
FORTUNE
5¢

"You will not go far because you are too
stupid to remove your overcoat."

"I live off the fat of the land too—I'm a diet counselor."

"And this is how we spent
our vacation . . ."

A TAKE
ON TRAVEL

"What are you going to do if you
actually catch something?"

"This is the last time I ride in coach!"

Baloo

*"I'd better be getting home now,
Herbert—my interest rate is dropping."*

ODD
COUPLES

MARRIAGE
COUNSELOR

Bucella

"Your wife says you never take her anywhere."

SCHWADRON

*"...and do you, single white male professional,
seeking companion for travel, theater, sports and
dining, take this single white female who desires
emotionally and financially secure interdependent
relationship, as your lawfully wedded wife?"*

Schneider

"Well, it's not my idea of a double date!"

SPORTING IDEAS

"Well, I think hang-gliding is a dumb idea."

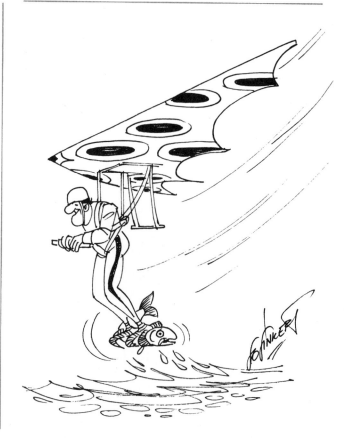

LAW ENFARCEMENT

"Wouldn't it be more dramatic if I fibbed a little so you could wring the truth out of me?"

"Now don't make him so mad that he doesn't try to make a deal."

"The witness will simply answer the question 'yes' or 'no'!"

"As I'm a law-abiding citizen, I thought you should know. . .your front wheel shows from the road."

NO KIDDING

"According to this, you are well-adjusted, properly motivated, cooperative, considerate, and flunking!"

"This time, you put on their coats, and I'll go honk the horn."

"Could I have a word with you?"

RUFF GOING

"Oh, about 2 blocks to a can of Alpo!"

"Not here, home."

"Can't you smile without sticking your tongue out?"

"The last time he brought my slippers, he tried to stuff them in my ear!"

YOU ARE WHAT YOU EAT

"Could I have the comic section?"

GLASBERGEN

"I am eating healthy! I'm having caffeine-free
pizza and sugar-free beer!"

Weyer

"Who told you spinach was loaded
with cholesterol?"

DELICATESSEN

COFFEE SHOP

BARBER SHOP

NO CHOLESTEROL

NO CAFFEINE

NO OPINIONS

JEANNE

TAX RELIEF

"Calvin is happiest when he has something unpleasant to look forward to."

"Of course we're middle class. We can't afford to buy anything, and nobody gives us anything."

"Sorry I'm late. They were auditing me."

"...so moved. We pool our tax cuts and send out for a pizza."

DRIVEN TO LAUGHTER

"... the good news is that we now have a phone in the car."

"How big is the purse this morning, Ed?"

"Call a plumber—the basement's full of water."

"Organ-donor card expired...."

PARLOR GAMES

*"Don't pay any attention, Monica—he's just upset
because you're sitting in his chair."*

"Why don't we just sit in the kitchen?"

"You rearranged the furniture again?"

"Notice anything different?"

SHADES OF GRAY MATTER

"Can I see you a minute, Sandburgh?"

"Remember! Don't grab it if it's hot!"

"I've been putting up with their insinuations that I'm a lousy math teacher for this many years!"

"We got the spot out."

IGNORING THE OBVIOUS

"We got into financial difficulties because
everything was so affordable."

"In addition, the house comes with a mulch pile."

"I did something wrong, didn't I?"

"May I ask who does your marketing research?"

VACATION DAZE

"But if you want our cheapest rate,
sir, we need somebody to ride on the wings
and keep the ice chipped off."

"I heard the national parks are crowded."

"Mother, Jason touched me again!"

"From what I hear, it's the most exclusive
beach in the entire state."

KIDS THESE DAYS

"Look what you've done to my father's car!"

"And they say kindergarten is only the beginning.... We could be looking at two or three more years!"

"My daughter tells me you're in show business."

"Twenty years from now you'll be telling some poor girl how delicious it was—so eat it!"

COTHAM CORNER

"Just let me know when the money's gone."

"I'll see to it you never work in this town again!"

"I have a challenging assignment for you, Robson! I
want you to go out and find another job."

TV GUIDES

"So try our product for 30 days; if not completely satisfied, try a different product."

"We'll return in a moment to 'One Life to Live.'"

DOUBLE TAKE

"According to your résumé you're my oldest son . . . could you elaborate on that?"

"Occupation? Dry cleaner."

IT'S ONLY MONEY

"The bad news is that the dollar has hit an all-time low—the good news is that nobody seems to have any."

"There are only two things you can count on—death and revenue enhancements."

"I'm from the Pentagon. We simply decided to eliminate the middleman!"

"No, Ed doesn't play; he bought them from neighbor kids that couldn't play either!"

CHILD PSYCHOLOGY

"My folks won't let me have any toy guns, but maybe we could work out some kind of secret arms deal."

"Ralph is very good with the children."

YOU DON'T SAY!

"You didn't? Who said you couldn't take it with you?"

"How's the cold?"

"No, having trouble parking is not considered a handicap."

ANIMAL CRACKERS

"Waiter, there's a hook in my soup."

"Kind of makes you feel inadequate, doesn't it?"

"Ketchup! How gross!"

"How long have you had these feelings of disorientation?"

"Unmitigated gall! What kind of diagnosis is that?"

"No, no! We attach the IV to the patient's wrist, nurse. We only bill them through the nose."

"MEDIC!"

"Call it a miracle if you want, but it could have been the 'Get Well' cards!"

"Your chart indicates good progress from the organ transplant, Mr. Goodrich."

ABOVE AND BEYOND

"You'll never guess how much money I made on the garage sale today!"

"I've told Ed to find your squeak—just let him ride around in your trunk for a few days."

"That's the last one I have in that size."

"We missed you this morning."

LOWLIGHTS OF HISTORY

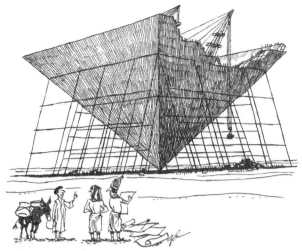

"I know it's none of my business, but could I make just one suggestion?"

"While you're up there, Orville, see what the traffic is like."

"Maybe it's just as well the artist didn't show after all."

"I only invented the darn thing yesterday, and this morning, Watson calls in sick!"

DOGGIE DEBACLES

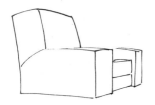

"You used the can opener—right, Martha?"

"He taught me to sit up, roll over, and beg, but I've never found any practical use for any of those things."

"Bad dog!"

AT A LOSS FOR WORDS

OUT IN LEFT FIELD

"Sorry, I'm not very good at names. Who am I anyway?"

"Mark my words, Frank, mark my words . . . one of these days I'm going to hop on this baby and keep right on going."

LIFE FROM ANOTHER PERSPECTIVE

"Don't sit too close, dear."

"We can withstand one charge, Ethel, but the second is sure to get us."

LEEWAY TO LAUGHTER

"Land ho!"

" 'scuze me, Cap'n,
but which way is it to the little
boys' poop deck?"

"Fred Biggs here—enjoying himself."

"Wait till you see what fishing does for your nerves, Ethel."

NOT ALWAYS AS THEY SEEM

OPTICAL ILLUSION EXHIBIT
ENTER HERE ←

MAN'S BEST FRIEND

"That's you, stupid!"

"He's just playing 'keep away'!"

TRUTH IN ADVERTISING

"Have fun, kids. . . . Oh, and Conrad,
it was so nice to meet you. You're exactly as
Joanne described you. . ."

". . .'better than nothing.'"

"Oh, but it is a duck dinner, sir.
Our duck simply adores it."

". . .And how long do you want
to borrow this student?"

MODERN-DAY MARCO POLOS

"You had to insist on the 'no-frills' cruise!"

*"Of course, if we don't hit the lottery
we'll have to cancel."*

WISE BEYOND THEIR YEARS

"Mind if I stroll leisurely alongside while you jog, dad?"

"You mean you didn't get your letter to Santa notarized?"

"A spelling test? Surely they have software for that sort of thing!"

"He can't sit up or heel, but he can turn on the television and open the refrigerator!"

FIDO FUN

"As I was saying...."

"Look here, Marge, I've taught Sparky to sit."

"I didn't like it!"

"That's that ding-a-ling Pavlov."

SIGN LANGUAGE

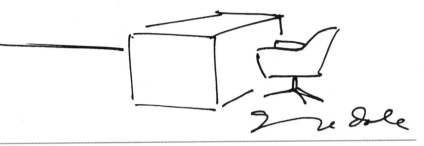

TORTS AND RETORTS

"I trust that the court's indiscriminate use of the phrase 'scum of the earth' will not unduly influence the jury in reaching a decision."

"Well, Your Honor, if a televised 1969 Perry Mason case isn't 'proper legal precedent,' I don't know what is!"

"We find the defendant guilty, but not as guilty as a lot of people."

R K BEMIS
ATTORNEY

CONSIDERED
OPINIONS $100.00

GUT REACTIONS $29.95

KID STUFF

"What did you expect? I barely have any education."

"No, ma'am, it ain't broke. Some guy gave me 50 bucks to keep his kids at the top for an hour!"

JIMMY PETERSON
ATE ALL HIS VEGETABLES

"So much for plea-bargaining."

BUREAU-CRACKS

ENGLEMAN.

GRINDALL

"My heart just wouldn't be in it with a $2.99 screwdriver!"

"The space program is simple— the government is looking for another planet to borrow money from."

"Electricity, The Saturday Evening Post and the Franklin stove are all right, but he doesn't like to talk about the U.S. postal service."

BASE LINES

"If they average .300 batting, they're heroes;
if we average .999 umpiring, we're bums."

"Who ordered the 'catch of the day'?"

"They lost."

"That looks like the top of the fifth, the count is three-and-two, bases are
loaded and the catcher is signaling for a curve ball, low and inside."

BON APPETIT

"On second thought, make that with onions."

"Come to think of it, what do bears like to eat?"

THAT'S MY BOY

CAPELINI

"Now that's what I call a real stupid place to give a guy a shot for a sore throat."

chon Day

"I hope this is just a phase you're going through."

McPherson

"I'm concerned about his thumb-sucking."

"Looks like Dad cleaned my room again."

Schochet

"Magazines . . . okay . . . we'll take them all!"

NOT WHAT YOU'D EXPECT

Rockwell

"I don't know. What do you think it is?"

WATER

WATER

WATER

WATER

Lem Grier

MIRRORS ON SALE
Some slightly irregular

noel

HAIR SPRAY

①

SSSSS

②

A PAWS IN THE ACTION

"It's been like this ever since she learned to work the can opener."

"When you leave, make sure the cat doesn't sneak out."

"Just what's your game?"

SNAKES, SNAILS, AND PUPPYDOG TAILS

"It turned out to be a real fun birthday party!"

"I'm going out in the yard to play."

"That was 'Apollo et Hyacinthus' by Mozart, written when he was 11."

"And this is where my mom pumps iron."

COUNTRY CAPERS

"It goes something like this: The early bird gets the worm, and then the early cat gets the early bird!"

"Better call the law, Pa! Cretins have landed in the south pasture!"

"See that, kid? That's good old natural food. Fresh young robin sprinkled with morning dew."

"I don't know how to break this to you, but I've got work to do."

PERSONNEL BUSINESS

"Can I take a message?
He's on the potty right now."

"Stop whimpering and spin the wheel, Hackworth!"

"I don't think it's wise for everyone to go
on a business trip at the same time!"

"Then again, I might be willing to consider
a smaller starting salary."

IT'S FOR THE BIRDS

"Sure, I look frazzled. Do you think it's easy selling penguins door-to-door?"

"If your father knew how bad you've been, he'd turn over in his gravy!"

"If you ask me, feeding them has just made them soft."

"I think you got the birdseed and the lawn fertilizer mixed up."

"Is it true, Mom—leftovers for the rest of my life?"

LIKE SANDS THROUGH THE HOURGLASS...

"Actually, I don't know how to act my age. I've never been my age before."

"Oh, sure. They all want to be grandmothers. Then as soon as you're pregnant, they retire to Florida."

"Me? Retired? Where did you get that idea? I just got a new boss, that's all!"

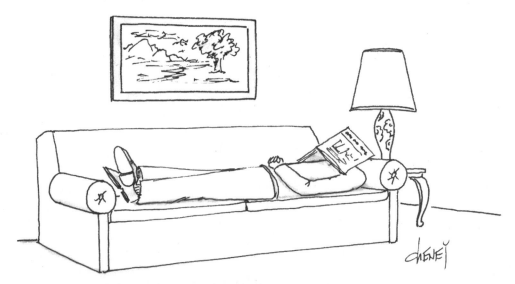

Martha and the kids having gone visting for the weekend, it wasn't long before Richard was up to his usual mischief.

SANTA AND OTHER CLAUSES

"If you can't sleep nights because of all the promises you made to those trusting little children ...I'd say it's time to quit the business."

"...and I want my husband to start helping with the housework, and my son to clean his room, and my mother to quit nagging me about my weight..."

"No! A ten-speed bike is out of the question, especially after what you did to Mrs. Peel's cat!..."

"You've been traded to another department store for six elves and an Easter bunny to be named later."

SAVING GRACE

"Of course they don't allow prayer in school—it's the one thing I'm good at!"

WREL
AMERICA'S
RELIGIOUS NETWORK

HEAVENLY   DIVINE   DEVILISH
HELLFIRE

"Is it okay for me to pray if
I go out in the hall?"

TELEVISION TRAUMA

"Now first of all, this is the guy
that sold us the camcorder."

"In a way, it's my fault...two years ago I told him,
'Oh, go ahead and be a macho, non-communicative
emotional hermit if that's what you want.'"

"When I was your age, I had to watch
whatever the networks put in front of me!"

VIDEOCASSETTE RECORDERS

"If we buy the more advanced model do you promise
you'll teach your mother and I how to operate it?"

IT'S A
WILD LIFE

"I was told this would be a casual affair."

*"Oh, no! There it is again! That awful
squishy feeling between my toes!"*

MATE
WANTED
DESPERATE
AND
SINCERE

"Don't be ridiculous! There's just one elephant up here."

LIFE ON THE LINKS

"I see the campaign for new
members has started..."

"You know what we need? We need some of
those colored golf balls."

"Great drive. Too bad about the
surface-to-air missile."

"The treasurer says that this is the best
investment the club ever made."

"It's a par 3 but the green is well-protected..."

CARAZY

"Those Japanese have gone too far this time!"

"Your car computer says it's the
battery, but my diagnostic computer says
it's the voltage regulator."

"Now, watch what happens when
I shift into second."

"Don't bother rotating the tires. They rotated on their own all the way here."

"I don't want a diet drink that tastes like lemons or grapes! I want a diet drink that tastes like pizza or cheeseburgers!"

"Honest! All I did was tap the bottle twice!"

SERVICE WITH A SMILE

"One hot dog—and will that be to go?"

"The kid's sunk a few bucks into promotion."

MODERN
MODEMS

"When he was a baby, his first words were 'momma' and 'data.'"

"Of course I got an 'F' in penmanship. I hardly write any more—I just type it in the computer."

"It's easy for you to say math isn't hard. They probably had fewer numbers when you were my age."

FOR THE RECORD

"Maybe there's only ten of them now, but just wait till the bureaucrats get to work."

Baloo

"Meanwhile, in Washington, D.C., credibility fell another seven points, reaching a new low for the year."

"...the same coffee maker used by the Air Force, now for the amazingly low price of $24.95! That's a savings of over $4,000.00!"

WILD WORLD OF SPORTS

"These tee-off times are getting ridiculous."

"I think it's terrific, but then I'm a sports fan."

GROWING PAINS

"You know, this town seemed so much
bigger when we were growing up!"

"Before we do our shopping,
son, there's a little something
your mother and I would like
to discuss with you."

"Everybody thinks I'm immature, except my mommy."

"Well, I'm eight and I don't understand 'em, either!"

LIKE CATS
AND DOGS

"I know what you mean. . .my claws get itchy just thinking about it."

"The ticking of the clock represents his mother's heartbeat. It's very reassuring to the puppy. No, dear, you're not supposed to set it."

"Leave 100 pounds of dog biscuits at the corner of Elm and South streets, or you'll never see your pipe and slippers again!"

"What on earth got you interested in reading that stuff?"

TRENDY TIMES

"Oh, Edward—not the Porsche
scarf with the BMW tie!"

"It was just a suggestion, sir. You don't have to
'have a nice day' if you don't feel like it."

"I'm afraid this is overdue,
but I was in a coma for a month."

"You heard me, buster! I said,
'Which room is the seminar in?'"

CHENEY'S
CHORTLES

"So...how are the time-travel experiments going?"

"Caution: Do not, under any circumstances, press the small, red button on top of the camera..."

"Quick! Back to your places—they just pulled into the driveway!"

"The jury is instructed to disregard the witness' last one-liner."

IF THOUGHTS COULD KILL

TECH–ED OFF

"It's about that tree in your
front yard—I just clocked it on my radar going 45
in a 25-mile-per-hour zone."

"Due to late-breaking technological advances,
please disregard your freshman year."

"How do I know that you aren't
just a weather balloon?"

"Unfortunately, the latest advances in medical technology
are not covered by your insurance company."

TROUBLE ON FOUR WHEELS

"Oh, she's a guzzler, alright!"

"I told you the front end of that
car stuck out too far!"

"Is this the wagon you advertised for $8,999?"

"Woman driver!"

SCIENCE FRICTION

"I'm convinced he's got one of those tiny TV sets in there."

"Things never change with the research-and-development boys. They always think they've found something that will solve all our problems."

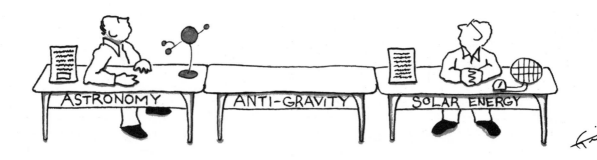

GREAT AND SMALL

"That's *Lassie?* That *little formation*
off the side of the cloud is Lassie? Look again, pal,
and I think you'll see Frank Sinatra."

"So you're ordering a dozen boxes of vanilla
creme-filled cookies and a dozen of the chocolate."

"Boscoe was indeed proud of himself for
guarding the car with keys still in ignition. However,
Boscoe had inadvertently discovered power locks."

"There's someone here to see you,
Howard. He said to mention a pet goldfish
you flushed down the toilet when
you were six years old."

INNINGS
& OUTINGS

"How was your day?"

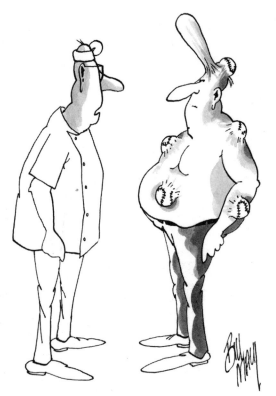

"It's baseball fever, Mr. Fisher...
you've caught it!"

375

"This is your last chance, kid...get your mind on
the game, or you're out of the line-up!"

"Fred and I are celebrating our 35th baseball season together."

THE DARNEDEST QUESTIONS

"How come it's wrong for you to do my homework, but it's right for me to do yours?"

"It's my professional opinion, Bill, that you can protect your baseball cards from Helen Garrett without a pre-going steady agreement!"

"If this is such a great story, how come they never made a sequel?"

"How could a mouse run up a clock?"

SM-ART ALECKS

"I love your painting, but who do you say did your framing?"

"Charles has very strong opinions when it comes to art."

"These three are some of his earliest works."

WARNING: THIS PAINTING HAS BEEN DETERMINED TO CAUSE EYE DAMAGE IN LABORATORY ANIMALS

XMAS X-CESS

"Would I be considered a kill-joy if I said
this is getting a bit ridiculous?"

"I assume there's a tree under there somewhere?"

"There must be a Santa Claus—
nobody could afford all this!"

"My dad's convinced Santa's a liberal Democrat!"

OUT OF BOUNDS

"And so, with the score 17 to 14, there's time-out on the field. I would remind you this is only a time-out, so don't go doing something stupid like sitting down to dinner."

"You didn't miss much—one millionaire caught the ball and another millionaire knocked him down."

"When Harry watches football, he likes a bit of atmosphere."

"I should caution you that the position you're applying for involves prolonged periods of boredom, punctuated with episodes of overwhelming chaos."

"When they *goof off*, they call it networking!"

"I'm warning you, Hotchworth, you're making a career decision, here!"

BUSINESS BUGABOOS

"But other than picketing our company in 1983, what other leadership traits have you shown?"

THANK HEAVEN I WAS ABLE TO SAVE THE DESK!

DOLLARS
AND
NONSENSE

VANFLEET

"I bet we could make these darn things five times the size if we made them hollow."

"Don't ask me how I know these things, Harry, just unload my Datatron Stock!"

"We try to keep a low overhead!"

Wilkie

MANY HAPLESS RETURNS

"When you said you were bringing a 'fat cat' home from the office, naturally I thought..."

"Boy, did I have a rough day."

"Bad day at the office, dear?"

"Gad, Rachel...what a day I've had. Is that collection of drunks from your office coming tonight, or tomorrow?"

VIEWER DISCRETION ADVISED

"He saw his first rerun today and thought he was cracking up!"

"I'm afraid we're going to have to tow it to the shop."

"Oh, no! Another one of those phony magicians!"

PHONE-Y BUSINESS

"Hello, operator? I was suddenly disconnected!"

"Who is it?"

"I've got to go. There's someone at the door!"

TEE FOR TWO

"His body English is the only exercise he gets out of golf."

"I always said when I make my pile I'm going to build a golf course all my own."

"Just follow the straight and narrow."

ATTITUDE ADJUSTMENTS

"We don't have any children of our own.
Fred is a school bus driver."

"Did I lose count on the number of scoops again?"

"Sir, Cunningham ate my carrot!"

"I thought a dog would cheer him up."

"You have a house in the suburbs, two
beautiful children, a devoted husband—what could you
possibly want with nuclear capability?"

LONG·TERM PARKING

DON'T BELIEVE IT

EARTH
ORBIT
THIS EXIT

1.

2.

3.

4.